3 KEYS TO UNLOCK
&
UNLEASH YOUR
CONFIDENCE

Samantha T. Mitchell

Before You Start Reading!

Scan this QR Code for a special and personal message from Samantha.

TABLE OF CONTENTS

INTRODUCTION

Are you going through life on autopilot? I can't be the only one who has ever arrived at a destination without much memory of the journey. We sometimes get so caught up that we don't enjoy the journey because we focus on the destination. Did you know that self-awareness and mindfulness can be a segue to a more confident you? Let's take a moment to think about what your life would look like if you had 10% more confidence.

If your mind is already racing, you have untapped greatness just waiting to be unleashed! Would you live a fulfilling life by doing more things that made you grow? Would your relationships, body image, health, wellness, and financial abundance improve with new choices?

The possibilities are endless, but it all starts when we learn to awaken our un-tapped potential by freeing ourselves from our limitations.

We all have the potential to compound our confidence; we just have to be brave enough to dig deeper.

Confidence is not about knowing all the answers - it's about being able to move forward knowing that you will figure it out. It's having that internal belief that you can handle whatever comes your way, even if it's a surprise. I can assure you that you will never feel 100% ready when you step outside your comfort zone. But just as routine stretching increases muscle flexibility, your confidence will also increase if you keep pushing beyond your limits.

Don't get me wrong. There is a difference between being confident and being fearless. We all have fears, but you need to manage them. Also, be aware that you can be confident in specific areas and not in others. I have yet to find anyone who is consistently confident in all aspects of life.

Being aware of our strengths is an essential tool for boosting your confidence. Not many of us have consciously taken time to understand our strengths. Once you know what these strengths are, you should work to remind yourself of them so you can boost them consistently.

Self-reflection can help you identify your strengths, and it can also be revealed by asking those you trust. Most of us are known for specific things, and our circle of influence can help highlight them if needed.

Repetition will increase your confidence. Think about when you first learned a specific task. Let's use cooking or baking for this example. The best chefs are highly confident in their craft. They practice certain dishes until they are perfected. You will always have control over competence-confidence because the more you practice, the higher your confidence will become.

Remember, muscle has memory! This book will give you the tools to compound your confidence with a Mindset, Behavior & Action (MBA) plan.

Let's highlight self-esteem and what it means because sometimes we can confuse it with confidence. Self-esteem is how positively you perceive your qualities and traits. This includes your physical appearance, abilities, achievements, values, beliefs, and how you think others view you.

One of my coaches described the difference: self-esteem is the *being*, and confidence is the *doing*. We will be focusing on the latter.

KEY # 1- MINDSET

Mindset is the first key. This key is unique to you, just as your fingerprint.

But, what exactly is mindset? Mindset is your mental attitude or set of beliefs that shape how you make sense of the world. This is the horsepower behind all our choices. Our mindset consists of conscious and subconscious beliefs that can go back as far as when you were in your mother's womb.

Our mindsets are based on survival. Your mind filters your daily experiences to increase your chances of survival. Now, let's dig deeper and take this to the next level. The personal trainer in me has to remind you that your mind is a perpetual learning machine. MINDFIT is known as mental stimulation that allows our minds to grow stronger, faster, and more efficiently, just as our muscles. It is always a work in progress.

MINDSET AND IDENTITY

So who are you, and how do you identify? I've learned that this is a question that most people struggle to answer also. I recall asking myself this question, and I struggled to come up with an answer. I could easily state my role in my career, but that lacked feeling, and I failed to make a real, meaningful connection.

This question is not like a question on a test that you crammed for. This is more like a practical exam that demonstrates that you have "practiced" your version of the game of life. What exactly are you practicing? You get to practice being within yourself. Your authentic self can be discovered when you spend time alone and ask the right questions. If we are never asked a question, our mind does not seek to answer it. Read that again!

It took me a while to grasp that concept. I validated that during my coaching sessions. I had a great coach who asked questions we sometimes don't even think to ask ourselves. When I'm asked the question, I typically dig to find some version of an answer that will be expanded upon later.

So let's dig deeper and begin our self-work. Ask yourself:

1. What does your ideal day look like? Who are you with? What do you feel?If you could craft your dream in your conscious state, what does it look like? Please remember to **focus on dreaming** and do not try to figure out how. The *how* is often a dream killer. We're manifesting here. Dream as BIG as your mind can imagine!

2. What is your passion? You are probably quick to say you don't know. Let's dig into this. Finding your passion is an inward journey, and it relies on looking at yourself and what you value in life.

You need to ask yourself what you love, what you enjoy doing, what you are good at, and how you can do more of it? Let's not make this a big project. Start small and work your way up. It's all about feeling here. You should feel excited and energized. And remember, these questions are interrelated. How you feel during your ideal day can help you find what you're doing when you feel your best and, therefore, what you're most passionate about. Answer the questions earnestly and let the outcomes flow organically.

Let's begin the journey to your identity. This isn't all about reading; you must do the self-work to experience true transformation. You're not afraid of a bit of work, though. Nah. You've been exercising along the way, right? You're more prepared for this next step than you think. Lean into your confidence zone and take the next step.

It took me years to figure out my passions, and I will honestly say that I didn't plan it. I made it plural for a reason. When I decided to get into aviation, it was a surprise to most. I just wanted a way to enjoy doing things with my hands. I enjoy figuring things out. I will say that exposure has everything to do with this process. You don't know what you don't know, after all.

My first airplane ride was when I was seven, and I first migrated to the US from Jamaica. I'm sure I thought it was cool, but I can't remember that far back. I do remember wondering how the airplanes were staying up in the air. Most adults are still amazed by this even with the scientific explanations, myself included. Airplanes were far from my mind when I was trying to decide on a career path, so I decided to become an auto mechanic.

That plan changed when I received a brochure from Vaughn College of Aeronautics as a senior in high school. That piece of paper changed my life. I started to imagine how cool it would be to be one of the contributors that helped with the most amazing form of travel. My imagination ran wild, and I felt like it was a sign, so I needed to act.

We all get signs!! Sometimes we ignore them. Some of these signs will show up multiple times if we don't follow through, but sometimes, we ignore the signs and miss the opportunity. Think about a time when you received a sign. Did you receive it, or did you let it go? If you let it go, did it show up again? My point is that there is no blueprint in life, but we get signs. When we become conscious of these signs and follow them, our lives can improve.

MINDSET AND LIMITING BELIEFS

What exactly is a limiting belief?

A limiting belief is a state of mind, conviction, or belief that you think to be true that limits you somehow. Limiting beliefs can have many negative effects. They could keep you from making good choices, taking new opportunities, or reaching your potential.

Let's take my example of being an aircraft mechanic for this. I was a female in a male-dominated industry! I'll keep it real here because I could have easily talked myself out of this. Since the industry was male-dominated and as much as I thought I was good with my hands, I had never been that close to an airplane besides when I was a passenger.

I'm not sure exactly what happened in my mind as all these limiting beliefs tried to take over, but I shifted my perspective.

I knew I wanted work, and I wanted options, so I told myself that any innovative employer would want a female on their team. I tapped into the fact that I would be bringing diversity to an industry that lacked it, which would be my leverage.

The bottom line here is that perspective is everything! It can shift your limiting beliefs that may otherwise hold you back.

PERFECTION KILLS DREAMS

I've always struggled with taking action. Everything had to be perfect, so things always moved slowly or not at all. This meant that I would sit on the sidelines and watch others take action. It took some self-reflection to figure out why I struggled with doing things "ugly." The answers are always within, but if we don't ask the right question, we will not get answers to help us grow.

I've worked in aviation for almost 20 years, an industry that is focused on first-time quality. My brain doesn't know the difference between aviation work-related tasks vs. other tasks. It generalized all my tasks. I'm not wired like most people because of how I've been trained. I have made a conscious effort to reprogram my brain to separate the tasks that need to be perfect the first time around and those that have room for imperfection.

This was a game-changer! I can officially say that striving for perfection doesn't stop me from delivering anymore. I'm perfectly imperfect, and I give myself permission to accept that honor humbly. I encourage you all to find strength in embracing the 85% solution...that is where the corners of opportunity to reshape, reform, innovate and evolve lie.

IMPOSTER SYNDROME

Imposter Syndrome is another dream killer. Have you ever found yourself questioning if you are good enough? I could easily say I'm an aerospace and fitness professional, so why do I think Ican become an author? I can because I've collected a series of experiences over the years, and writing a book is how I can help others.

You don't have to go through the same struggles if I share my experiences. The struggles don't even have to be the same. I'm here to compress what took me decades to learn in one super succinct book.

So how do we get rid of limiting beliefs and imposter syndrome? The first step is to acknowledge them. We have to spend some quiet time with ourselves again. What stories are you telling yourself? Here are a few examples of some of my favorites:

- I'm not enough. I bought myself a ring with "I am Enough" on it as a constant reminder of who I am, what I stand for, and what I bring to the table (and yes, I can BRING the table if needed) is ALWAYS enough.

- XXX {Insert whatever you want XXX to be} is not for people like me.

- People that look like me can't achieve XXX.

- I don't have enough time. (This has to hit home for someone reading this.)

- I don't have enough money. One of my favorite quotes to counteract this is, "You don't lack resources. You lack resourcefulness" ~Tony Robbins.

- Love is painful. Are you using conscious or subconscious generalizations about love based on past experiences?

Once we acknowledge our limiting beliefs and their roots, we are almost there. Next, we need to plant some new seeds in our mental garden. Remember, seeds do not grow overnight, so we need to be patient. Let's begin planting. For each limiting belief, we will replace it with an empowering one. For example, *I do not have enough time* can be replaced with *I am committed to scheduling time to focus on that specific priority.*

AFFIRMATIONS

This is where our affirmations will come into play.

Write out and repeat your affirmations at least three times a day. That sounds like work, right? The growth journey requires work! I promise the harvest is well worth it, though. Remember, you must believe and feel these, so don't just list meaningless things. If you don't believe it, find a few that you believe in, then start and build on that.

It would be best if you were to be connected with them daily. I remember when I first realized that affirmations worked. I found a 21-day financial abundance daily affirmations program, and let me tell you.... abundance became my birthright! Money started flowing in from both expected and unexpected ways. The more you believe, the better your delivery. But as I stated before, be patient. Water your soil with commitment to the task, and remember, the best crops are produced after a season of nurture and care.

KEY # 2 - BEHAVIORAL PATTERNS OF THE CONFIDENT YOU

How does your behavior impact your confidence?

Confidence develops when you have a deep sense that you can handle the emotional outcome of whatever you are facing or pursuing. We are emotional creatures, so we need to address how we feel or will feel with a specific result. If we knew we were guaranteed success, we could easily say we were confident. Sorry to be the bearer of bad news, but we can never fully guarantee success. Sometimes the road to success is not how we planned it, but we win at life when we can receive whatever comes and still persevere.

Then there is the "fake it until you make it approach." This is precisely how you gain confidence. Keep showing up and playing the role until it becomes natural.

I've read so many books stating that the mind doesn't know what's real and what's imagined. It took me a while to realize that this was true. When I got my first job in commercial aviation, I was not confident in being an aircraft mechanic.

Heck, I was scared! I studied hard in school and did all the practical courses, but the real thing is a whole different ball game.

Remember when I said there would be opportunities for women in this industry? There were plenty. I was the first female mechanic to work for Air Jamaica out of JFK in New York. I knew some people wanted me to fail, and a few wanted to see me win. I started focusing on all those who wanted to see me succeed. After having a heart-to-heart discussion with myself, I decided that this was my journey, and I knew it started with me.

I hung on to the few that wanted to see me succeed, but I had to remind myself daily that I was the number one person rooting for me. I became my own cheerleader because I refused to let those dudes see me sweat. Becoming my own cheerleader came at a cost. I had to put in extra work and seek help from anyone willing to teach me.

At the time, my coworker, Rae, had a vested interest in seeing me win. I was unclear why he was one of the few who wanted to work with me, so I asked him why. He told me that he wanted someone new to work with and that he wanted help! He knew I was trainable. I wasn't like all the other new people that came who acted like they knew everything. I guess I faked it enough to gain support and, shortly after, made it.

I worked third shift because that's when the airplanes were not flying, and there was one night that I will never forget.

I gave myself the usual pep talk before work, but I got paired up with someone who did not want to see me win. He wanted to see me fall flat on my face. We were assigned to the biggest aircraft in our fleet, an A340. It's a four-engine aircraft. Huge! The tires are almost as tall as me, and one needed to be changed. My partner for the night told me to do it.

After a slight panic attack, I paused and thought to myself that none of the other guys would do that job alone. So I found Rae and worked with him that night and left the other guy alone to tap into his resources to get the job done.

The tire was changed that night, but I didn't do it. I'm sure he was pissed, but I didn't care; he asked for an egg on his face. I celebrated that I leveraged my resourcefulness to complete other tasks that night with a partner who wanted to see me grow. This would prove to be a pivotal moment for my confidence, which was elevating.

INTERNAL VS. EXTERNAL VALIDATION

As human beings, we all want to feel loved. Everyone wants to be liked. They seek external validation for fulfillment. This is why social media has taken over.

What if I told you external validation would never fulfill you if you are not fulfilled within? My lack of internal validation kick-started my personal development journey and entrepreneurship journey. It began after my husband, and I had our second daughter. The snapback was not as grand as when I was in my twenties. I was 'fluffier' than I was before getting pregnant. I call it fluff because that's precisely what it was.

It's always funny to hear my husband tell the story of how everything started. He used to love to take me shopping for really fancy dresses. One day, the experience was not like he expected. It took longer than usual, and I still wasn't totally thrilled with my purchase. Little did I know that I just wasn't happy with myself and my body image at the time.

I got all dressed up, did my hair and makeup, and stepped out for a family wedding. Hair and makeup were beautiful, so I was feeling myself until I was approached by a family member who commented on my weight. Let's just agree that just because you have a thought, you shouldn't articulate it without thinking about the impact it may have. I felt like crap the rest of the night because of her words. Her words ruined my night because I wasn't secure within myself, so a slight jab left a significant scar. I tried to act as if nothing had happened, but that was extremely hard, and my husband noticed. I shared what happened, and he did what any loving husband would do - he consoled his wife. This night was a significant pivot in my journey because if my self-esteem had been higher, the words would not have been that powerful.

Has there been a time when words stung more because of what you thought about yourself and your self-worth? Was it the words, or was it your insecurities that made the stinging worse? I knew I wanted to get to where the most important words were mine, but I wasn't sure how. This is where I began my health and fitness journey as a lifestyle.

This journey was not only about my nutrition and my workouts, but I also joined a community that focused on personal development. It was the tool that I used to reduce the impact of other people's opinions of me.

One of my favorite Jack Canfield quotes that I hold near and dear to my heart is, "What others think about you is none of your business." When we get to the place of self-love and self-acceptance, this is when we can truly embrace the meaning behind this quote.

COMPOUNDED CONFIDENCE

It's always exciting to think about transformation, but it's even more exciting to witness it. Let's begin with an exercise. You will not need any weights for this. Write out what you would do with 10% more confidence in the following areas of your life:

RELATIONSHIPS

With 10% more confidence, I will find creative ways to have open dialogue with my husband because I strive to maintain healthy relationship boundaries.

All relationships require work, and we should strive to be conscious about contributing to the growth or decline of our relationships.

I got creative and learned that there would not be any weird expectations if I communicated well. For example, my husband and I work, so I learned to share that making dinner was far from my mind if I knew my work schedule would be nuts. That doesn't make me a bad person, and I have zero guilt. If I have a problem and don't say anything, it stays my problem. If I share the problem, now it's not only mine—genius how this works.

What will you do with 10% more confidence?

Now let's pause and visualize this happening. What are you hearing, seeing, and feeling? You may be asking yourself, what next? How do I get my 10%? This is where ACTION comes into play. Do it, and you will feel yourself growing. Once you have completed this task, you have officially increased your confidence. If you like to play big, you can go for **Compounded Confidence** by repeating the cycle.

Before you repeat, be sure to celebrate your 10% ROY (Return on Yourself). Celebrate myself? What does that mean? Go on a big vacation? Treat yourself to an elaborate dinner? It took me a while to clarify what it means to celebrate myself. I finally gained clarity while writing this book on how I really like to celebrate; I love to share my success with those in my tribe.

I specifically call out my tribe because they understand the rules of this journey and will allow me to be my authentic self without judgment or criticism. Just like me, discover how you enjoy being celebrated and do so often and openly.

Finances

With 10% more confidence, I made it my personal goal to increase my annual income by 25%. Now it's your turn. Remember, you don't have to know the how. Just identify what you would do with the increased confidence.

You can achieve goals you never thought possible by simply asking and putting them out into the universe. With the right mindset, you will attract opportunities and connections to help you to achieve your goal. All you need to do is believe in it.

As you work on this goal, continue your affirmations. Feel free to add specific affirmations that are tied to financial abundance. One of my favorites is, "Money comes to me easily and effortlessly." Repetition is key for this to be effective, so set your reminders. This is a financial goal, so celebrate and shoot for **Compounded Confidence** by repeating this after you hit that goal.

Physical Body and Body Image

Wow...

I think all my ladies will smile just by thinking about this one. What would you do with 10% more confidence that is centered around your body image? Is there a dress that you already have that you would love to wear confidently?

Let's connect with this on a visual level. See yourself in the state that you desire. I'm rocking that bodycon dress with no sleeves to showcase my arms and back. What are you doing? Visualize it and feel what you feel with that accomplishment. Celebrate yourself as if it's happening. Enjoy the moment.

Health and Wellness

Are there health and wellness activities that will help you reach your goals? We have to be in good health to achieve our life goals. This goes beyond your body image. For example, my health and wellness goal is maintaining acceptable levels for my annual health screening.

Fear of Failure or Fear of Success

Our brains are wired to keep us safe; it likes our comfort zone.

Unfortunately, this isn't where our greatness happens because remember how this all started? It started with the idea that if we had more confidence, we would have the ability to do more, which naturally means there is more within us.

Therefore, if you stick to your comfort zone, you will limit yourself and never achieve full growth. So let's examine the "F" word. I've wanted to do many things in the past, but I allowed FEAR (The big nasty "F" bomb) to hold me back. If you can relate to this, keep reading (even if you can't, KEEP READING!). There is a light at the end of the tunnel. I say tunnel because we are limited by what we allow ourselves to see if we have tunnel vision.

Let's put this into perspective with a real-life example. I realized that I was afraid of speaking in large crowds. What was my fear? I was comfortable with my content, so it wasn't that. After analyzing the root of the fear, I realized I was afraid of other people's perceptions. Go figure! It doesn't matter how old we are; we all seek some form of approval.

I questioned whether my audience would agree with my thoughts and insights. Would my story inspire them? This was a mind-blowing discovery. After realizing what was holding me back, I had to do some self-work. I asked myself if there was a particular person that I feared rejection from, or was it, everyone? I later asked myself if I would be happy to impact only one person positively.

This was where my shift happened. I focused on one person instead of everyone. My success became planted in the impact of one person, not my potential failure for not resonating with the masses. Now it's your turn.

What is something you know that makes you fearful? Spend some time thinking about what that true fear is. Once you identify the root, decide if it's something worth keeping. What's the cost of keeping it versus the value of letting it go? Letting go doesn't mean that it is totally gone; it simply means that you are managing it.

During one of my coaching calls, I learned that "fear is basically the green light to go." I'm not telling you to do anything dangerous, but when it's something that aligns with your growth, feel the fear and do it anyway.

Fear shows up when we want to grow, when things are unfamiliar - when we are more committed to *unfamiliar discomfort vs. familiar discomfort*. It's all about stretching ourselves. Sometimes when we need a good stretch, we need help from a coach or accountability partner. And that is OK. If you need help overcoming fears and being held accountable, use your resources just as I did in my tire-changing example. Use your circle of influence to help you grow and become better.

Morning Routines

It's all about how you start your day. Your morning routine sets the expectations for your day. We all have our own version, but the magic happens when we follow it consistently. I have done a few iterations of my morning routines over the years, and I can say that when I have a solid morning routine, my days are definitely better.

This doesn't mean that all of my days are perfect. A solid morning routine prepares me mentally so I can handle things that come my way with a better perspective. After all, it's not what happens to you but how you react that shows growth as an individual.

My best morning routine was after I completed the *Unleash the Power Within* workshop with Tony Robbins. I had to wake up at 4:30 AM to do everything, but I admit, I was on such an internal high that it didn't matter. My routine consists of priming, which includes some movement, breathing, gratitude, and goal visualization. I still practice it to this day because it works well for me. It's all about finding something that you can commit to consistently.

Gratitude

It's so easy to get lost in the daily grind of life and focus on the negative and the bad things that make life challenging. Sometimes we forget to think about and appreciate the positive; some may take it for granted. I can see your confidence surging ahead when you realize what a great life you have.

Making gratitude a daily practice is a great way to elevate your confidence. There is no limit to the number of things you can be grateful for, small or big. You can choose to write it down or verbally state what you are grateful for daily. This can shift your attitude for the better.

Developing your attitude for gratitude can increase your confidence, and you will realize that you truly have a great life.

Note that I said, great, not perfect. I've learned to embrace that I'm only perfect at being imperfect. There is no such thing as a perfect life; life is all about the perspective that you choose to focus on.

Celebrating Yourself

Celebrate yourself for coming this far in your journey of self-discovery.What is celebrated, gets repeated. I've always said adults are three-year-olds with a lot more responsibilities and dire consequences. Think about how your three-year-old self would repeat what got celebrated. We often take all our great work for granted. This is especially true in high achievers. They expect it from themselves, so they don't celebrate their achievements.

This is an area of opportunity for most, so I challenge you to start your celebration journal. It's evidence that you are working on yourself and making progress. We tend to forget all the cool things we do. Let's not take our accomplishments for granted; we put in a lot of work for the win. Small wins compound over time, so be sure to add this to your daily routine. We are subconsciously creating our winning mindset, so let's start now.

Mirror Work

If you want more, mirror exercises are for you. This is a game-changer for those who are ready to connect with themselves on a higher level. By saying affirmations in front of the mirror, you can plant seeds of belief in your mind. With time and enough affirmations, you will begin to feel more comfortable in your skin. This, in turn, will stop you from looking for imperfections in your body.

With time, the practice will become involuntary. You will not avoid mirrors or storefront windows because you hate the way you look. You will actually seek them out and preen yourself in front of them. With an increase in self-esteem, that negative voice inside your head will disappear.

The ideal time for this exercise is first thing in the morning to set the tone for your day and, at night, to close out your day. Most people will notice a difference in you within a week of doing this exercise. But make sure you stick to it for at least a month to get optimal results.

Here is how you can do this exercise and maximize its efficiency:

- Take a few deep diaphragmatic (belly) breaths.
- Smile - *This is the only exercise I'll ask you to do. Research shows that smiling can reduce stress and release endorphins.*
- Repeat some positive affirmations that you connect with most. Here are a few of my favorites:
    - I am proud of who I am and who I am becoming.
    - I am an abundant leader who shares her light with others.
    - I radiate confidence in all that I do.
    - I am doing great things with my life.
    - I trust myself.
    - I am making the right choices for the divine assignment on my life
    - Today is going to be a great day *(Declare it in the AM)*
- Celebrate your wins during the PM or declare the wins you want for AM
    - I, **Name,** celebrate you for (placeholder). Small wins count, so don't forget them.
- Forgive yourself - *This can go back as far as you wish.*
    - I, **Name,** forgive you for (placeholder).
      WARNING - This can be emotional for some.
- Tell yourself that you love all of you. Enjoy the moment of self-love.

KEY #3 – ACTION

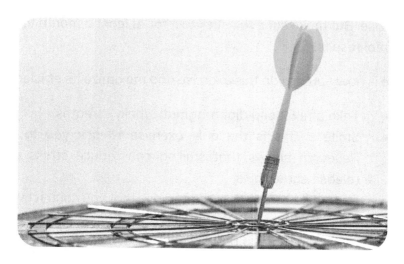

A ction brings more clarity than thought. I have tried to plan things from beginning to end, but I've learned over the years that we find answers by doing.

Try activating your action muscle to manage your fears, minimize procrastination and yield the outcome you want. It will feel weird and uncomfortable at first, but repetition is the key to success. If something gets repeated enough, I guarantee you will feel more confident in doing it.

How do you take action when that annoying voice in your head starts to ask questions and drives your self-doubt and fear? We **ALL** experience this, but we all handle it differently.

When the questions come up, ask yourself one simple question, "What's the worst that can happen?" This should shift your perspective and allow you to take action if you have a strong enough why. Let's face it, we want a lot of things, but we are not willing to work for everything. Let's filter out what we are willing to work for.

Shift to an abundance mindset and watch how you attract abundance.

One of my favorite Tony Robbins quotes is, "Where focus goes, energy flows." We must consciously shift our focus to get what we want.

PREPARATION FOR SUCCESS

Have you ever had to host an event, do a speech, or a presentation? As you prepare for these events, you are working your confidence muscle.

A few years ago, I remember I was asked to MC the fall fashion show for Athleta. It was indeed an honor to be selected, but the negative voices were renting space in my head. I've done tons of presentations and speeches at work, but this one was outside of my comfort zone, so I had to evict the negative thoughts that were popping up in my head.

I prepared differently because I knew this would require turning up the dial on my internal thermostat. My comfort zone operates at about 70 degrees, and this was putting me about 10-15 degrees higher. I could have easily said no because I had never done a fashion show before, but I accepted the challenge.

This is what I learned. Nervousness goes away at some point, and you get to be your authentic self. I prepared, showed up nervous, had fun and it turned out to be a successful evening. I share this because I stretched myself with this opportunity, and I want to show you what is possible when you do the work. My action muscle was in full activation. Let's put yours to work!

THE TRUTH BEHIND PROCRASTINATION

Let's jump into procrastination because I know I'm guilty of not doing things I commit to doing too. We each have different stories on why we procrastinate.

Why do we do this to ourselves? Most of us do it because we lack clarity in our priorities, feel overwhelmed, or feel inadequate for a specific task. We often procrastinate with things that are optional vs. things that are non-negotiable.

Most of us are expert procrastinators because we feel safe doing it. I attended a group coaching call where we spoke about our egos. My coach, Sean Smith and Danita Sajous, highlighted that our ego's primary commitment is to protect our self-image, not make our self-image positive, helpful, or feel good.

In other words, our ego should protect whatever self-image we already have. For example, if your self-image is unlovable, your ego works full time to make you feel unlovable. This is why our self-work is layers deep – we need to heal our inner child first or we will always fall prey to our ego.

So let's take your image of being unlovable first. Ask yourself, what will the ego do in a loving relationship? Our ego will self-sabotage to protect that self-image or belief about ourselves, which is not valid. Can you think of a time when you self-sabotaged due to your thoughts?

I can think back to when I started this journey, and I believed that I had to be perfect. I had to be the perfect coach to have a lot of clients. But I quickly realized that clients don't want perfection; they want someone who is relatable. They want another human being with specific skill sets that they can connect with.

The pressure to win can also drive procrastination. Was there a time when you wanted to succeed at something specific but the fear of not winning prevented you from taking action? Ouch... I think we can all relate to this.

I was deep in my personal development journey, and an "opportunity" popped up. I was online one night, and an ad popped up to do a competition for Ms. Health and Fitness. The first thought that popped into my head was, really? But, I decided to do it anyway and see what would happen. I entered this 6-week challenge and started promoting what I was doing to solicit support from friends and family.

Everyone was super supportive, and I won the first few rounds easily. This competition put me at 100+ degrees on my comfort thermostat. I consistently asked for support because I knew I couldn't win alone. I reconnected with people that I hadn't spoken to in years. Easy right? Nope. As the rounds progressed, I quickly learned that asking for "free" votes was not enough. I now needed to solicit donations to increase my chances of winning. This was painful because one of the things I hate the most is asking for money. I had a decent morning ritual going before starting the competition, but I had to level up my mindset further as the competition got further along.

I quickly learned that I needed to be in peak state for the rest of the competition. Even when I was in peak state, I would still get frustrated. I would often hear, "Sam, you already know you will win." I knew that behind the scenes, my contribution to my community or physical conditioning had absolutely nothing to do with winning. Winning was a direct result of votes, and I knew I didn't know enough people in the world to only focus on free votes or anything less than three figures.

Yikes!! It is nuts to type this now. I wanted to quit so bad, but I was so far along, and I learned that winning wasn't about me. I learned that others were cheering me on for doing something on a large scale. It somehow represented something that they wanted to do, but never acted upon so in a sense, they were living through me.

I was sharing my light with so many people so, despite wanting to stop, I knew that it wasn't an option. I got large donations from people I had never met. There were days when I had to pause to reflect on why I was where I was. The journey was stressful, but the support often took away most of the stress.

I was trying to win Ms. Health and Fitness, and my blood pressure was high. My doctor wanted to put me on medication, but I told him it would be over soon and that I would regulate it without prescription medication.

During the last week of the competition, I got to a point where I was 3rd and stayed there for a few days. Family and friends were still rooting, but I knew that to win 1st would be at a very high price, and I had already won.

I won by being a part of the journey, meeting new friends, reconnecting with old friends, and by getting love and support over a six-week process. To this day, some people tell me that they voted every day. That alone fills me up. I did get featured for placing 3rd, which was a surprise, but I actually won when I made a conscious decision to go on the journey. So you can minimize procrastination by increasing your self-awareness. If you learn why you procrastinate and how to deal with it, you will automatically free up time to take action on what matters. Always start with what motivates you, then take those micro action steps, and celebrate so you can reinforce your drive to keep going. Small actions will compound over time.

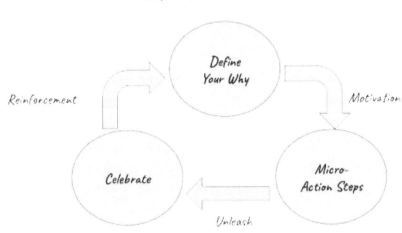

3-Steps to Combat Procrastination

INCREASED COMPETENCE

Practice your way to confidence.

If you want to be a better speaker, speak more. It takes time, and always remember to not compare your journey with someone who is chapters ahead of you. Only compare yourself to the previous versions of yourself. We often forget to be kind to ourselves as we increase our competence level.

Think back to when you learned to walk. How many tries did it take? You probably have no clue unless you are superhuman. Babies do not keep tabs on their number of attempts; they only know the outcome they want. They stop when they have achieved results. I'm usually all for metrics, but there are some instances where we should ditch the numbers and focus on getting what we want. I dare you to try it. You will see a visible difference in your confidence levels for sure.

Once you increase your competence, you will notice that others will also want to celebrate you. One of the biggest lessons I've learned and what I am actively still working on is accepting compliments. I used to shrug them off because I didn't think I deserved them.

After increasing my awareness, I realized that the habit was self-defeating. I didn't believe in what I did, so I struggled to accept praises from others. The first step before changing is always awareness. After I realized what was going on, I had to learn to say thank you and embrace the fact that my efforts were worthy of recognition. If you struggle with this too, give this a try.

FAILURE IS FEEDBACK

How many times have you not taken action because you feared failure? Did you notice that the regret you felt later was as haunting as the failure itself? I had to teach both my conscious and subconscious that failure is simply just feedback.

I'm a huge Apple fan, and they are always doing software updates. Would I need to do multiple updates if they had a perfect product? If one of the top-ranked companies in the world can upgrade, why can't I? Once I shifted to this mindset, a whole new world opened up for me.

I remember when I first started investing at 18 years of age. I was in the banking industry, so I decided to participate in everything we offered. I invested $1000 in some mutual funds and lost almost all of it.

This was an expensive lesson, especially at such a young age but it taught me a valuable lesson.

I learned that I needed to do more research instead of simply relying on someone else's advice. The advice may have been valid, but they never taught me an exit strategy, and I didn't know I needed one. Fast forward to today, and I always build in an exit strategy for gains and losses.

TRUST YOURSELF

Trust that you are ready for the next level of elevation that awaits you. When we learn to shut out the noise, we can hear even better. Continue to do your daily self-work to build self-trust. These tools and practices are meant to get you through the difficult times, as well as celebrate the good times.

Let's give ourselves permission to become aware of our thoughts and feelings while working on unleashing the best version of ourselves. The question is, do you trust that YOU have the power to create and sustain the best version of YOU?

CONCLUSION

The keys to unlocking and unleashing your confidence are all in the hands of the person reading this book. You are equipped with the tools you need to help you, but the true transformation comes from self-work.

This is a journey, so be sure to give yourself grace and ease. Treat this like when you first learned to walk; if you fall down, try again. There is no limit to how many tries you get. You can try for as long as you need to; you are the lead actor/actress in your own movie. Always remember, start before you are ready because if you wait until you are ready, it's already too late.

Let's continue the journey of unlocking and unleashing your confidence. Let me see you flex!

ABOUT THE AUTHOR

Samantha Mitchell is a wife, mother of two, the founder of Confidence MBA, health coach, Anytime Fitness franchisee, Mrs. Delaware 2019, Ms. Health & Fitness top 3 2021, and 20+ year aerospace professional. She's coached her clients on both nutrition and personal training; however, she realized that true transformation is centered around mindset or, as we now know, *mindfit.*

Mindset is the foundation for any transformation in all aspects of life. She founded Confidence MBA through her personal journey to mindset transformation coupled with her corporate experiences as a black female in a male-dominated industry. She strives to create a movement to let others know that they are not alone and that we all can turn up the dial on our confidence thermostat with the right tools and strategies. A few degrees can kick-start the creation of your legacy, increase financial abundance, improve relationships, and improve your overall quality of life. The possibilities are endless.

Samantha was blessed with her rebirth in the middle of the COVID-19 pandemic. There were a lot of negatives with the pandemic, but it was also an opportunity to slow down and grow. She began to deepen her inner work growth and development after feeling a sense of emptiness.

She was on a quest for something, not knowing what "something" was. Samantha later learned that it was a more profound sense of self-love and self-discovery. She asked the universe for guidance and was connected with Lisa Nichols and the Motivating the Masses coaches. This was the foundation of her rebirth, along with the connection with her tribe and her family and friends.

It's essential to build your tribe if you don't have one. Always remember, your tribe is your vibe! What vibes are you sending? Invest in yourself; go to the seminar, take the course, and network with like-minded people.

SPECIAL BONUS OFFER

As a thank you for purchasing the 3 Keys to Unlock and Unleash your Confidence, Samantha Mitchell is offering you a free Confidence MBA introductory coaching session, redeemable at

www.confidencemba.com. This session will activate your self-discovery button and initiate clarity on your personalized Confidence MBA plan. You will leave your call empowered to activate your transformational journey to elevate your mindset to become the best version of yourself. That's a total value of $199 — for free!

I understand the importance of your tribe, so I'm also sharing this same offer with two people in your tribe to elevate the confidence levels in your circle. I call it the trifecta!

CONFIDENCE MBA 30-DAY CHALLENGE

Transformation requires implementation, so please join me for our 30-day Confidence MBA challenge. Let's write out what you will do with 10% more confidence in the various areas of your life.

1. What would you do with 10% more confidence in the area of your relationships?

_____

_____

2. What would you do with 10% more confidence in the area of your finances?

_____

_____

3. What would you do with 10% more confidence in the area of your physical body and body image?

_____

_____

4. What would you do with 10% more confidence in the area of health and wellness?

_____

_____

DAILY CHALLENGE ACTIVITY

Complete the following for the next 30 days. As you go through each day, remember no one has the power to dim the light that shines from within you. Let your light shine unapologetically!

DAY 1

Affirmations - I AM:

_____

_____

Today I am grateful for:

_____

_____

Today I aim to:

_____

_____

Today I will practice self-care by:

_____

_____

Today I celebrate myself for:

_____

_____

I forgive myself for:

_____

_____

Day 2

Affirmations - I AM:

_____

_____

Today I am grateful for:

_____

_____

Today I aim to:

_____

_____

Today I will practice self-care by:

_____

_____

Today I celebrate myself for:

_____

_____

I forgive myself for:

_____

_____

Day 3

Affirmations - I AM:

_____

_____

Today I am grateful for:

_____

_____

Today I aim to:

_____

_____

Today I will practice self-care by:

_____

_____

Today I celebrate myself for:

_____

_____

I forgive myself for:

_____

_____

Day 4

Affirmations - I AM:

_____

_____

Today I am grateful for:

_____

_____

Today I aim to:

_____

_____

Today I will practice self-care by:

_____

_____

Today I celebrate myself for:

_____

_____

I forgive myself for:

_____

_____

Day 5

Affirmations - I AM:

_____
_____

Today I am grateful for:

_____
_____

Today I aim to:

_____
_____

Today I will practice self-care by:

_____
_____

Today I celebrate myself for:

_____
_____

I forgive myself for:

_____
_____

Day 6

Affirmations - I AM:

_____

_____

Today I am grateful for:

_____

_____

Today I aim to:

_____

_____

Today I will practice self-care by:

_____

_____

Today I celebrate myself for:

_____

_____

I forgive myself for:

_____

_____

Day 7

Affirmations - I AM:

_____
_____

Today I am grateful for:

_____
_____

Today I aim to:

_____
_____

Today I will practice self-care by:

_____
_____

Today I celebrate myself for:

_____
_____

I forgive myself for:

_____
_____

Day 8

Affirmations - I AM:

_____

_____

Today I am grateful for:

_____

_____

Today I aim to:

_____

_____

Today I will practice self-care by:

_____

_____

Today I celebrate myself for:

_____

_____

I forgive myself for:

_____

_____

Day 9

Affirmations - I AM:

_____
_____

Today I am grateful for:

_____
_____

Today I aim to:

_____
_____

Today I will practice self-care by:

_____
_____

Today I celebrate myself for:

_____
_____

I forgive myself for:

_____
_____

Day 10

Affirmations - I AM:

_____

_____

Today I am grateful for:

_____

_____

Today I aim to:

_____

_____

Today I will practice self-care by:

_____

_____

Today I celebrate myself for:

_____

_____

I forgive myself for:

_____

_____

Day 11

Affirmations - I AM:

_____
_____

Today I am grateful for:

_____
_____

Today I aim to:

_____
_____

Today I will practice self-care by:

_____
_____

Today I celebrate myself for:

_____
_____

I forgive myself for:

_____
_____

Day 12

Affirmations - I AM:

Today I am grateful for:

Today I aim to:

Today I will practice self-care by:

Today I celebrate myself for:

I forgive myself for:

Day 13

Affirmations - I AM:

_____

_____

Today I am grateful for:

_____

_____

Today I aim to:

_____

_____

Today I will practice self-care by:

_____

_____

Today I celebrate myself for:

_____

_____

I forgive myself for:

_____

_____

Day 14

Affirmations - I AM:

_____

_____

Today I am grateful for:

_____

_____

Today I aim to:

_____

_____

Today I will practice self-care by:

_____

_____

Today I celebrate myself for:

_____

_____

I forgive myself for:

_____

_____

Day 15

Affirmations - I AM:

_____
_____

Today I am grateful for:

_____
_____

Today I aim to:

_____
_____

Today I will practice self-care by:

_____
_____

Today I celebrate myself for:

_____
_____

I forgive myself for:

_____
_____

Day 16

Affirmations - I AM:

_____

_____

Today I am grateful for:

_____

_____

Today I aim to:

_____

_____

Today I will practice self-care by:

_____

_____

Today I celebrate myself for:

_____

_____

I forgive myself for:

_____

_____

Day 17

Affirmations - I AM:

_____
_____

Today I am grateful for:

_____
_____

Today I aim to:

_____
_____

Today I will practice self-care by:

_____
_____

Today I celebrate myself for:

_____
_____

I forgive myself for:

_____
_____

Day 18

Affirmations - I AM:

_____

_____

Today I am grateful for:

_____

_____

Today I aim to:

_____

_____

Today I will practice self-care by:

_____

_____

Today I celebrate myself for:

_____

_____

I forgive myself for:

_____

_____

Day 19

Affirmations - I AM:

_____

_____

Today I am grateful for:

_____

_____

Today I aim to:

_____

_____

Today I will practice self-care by:

_____

_____

Today I celebrate myself for:

_____

_____

I forgive myself for:

_____

_____

Day 20

Affirmations - I AM:

_____

_____

Today I am grateful for:

_____

_____

Today I aim to:

_____

_____

Today I will practice self-care by:

_____

_____

Today I celebrate myself for:

_____

_____

I forgive myself for:

_____

_____

Day 21

Affirmations - I AM:

_____
_____

Today I am grateful for:

_____
_____

Today I aim to:

_____
_____

Today I will practice self-care by:

_____
_____

Today I celebrate myself for:

_____
_____

I forgive myself for:

_____
_____

Day 22

Affirmations - I AM:

_____

_____

Today I am grateful for:

_____

_____

Today I aim to:

_____

_____

Today I will practice self-care by:

_____

_____

Today I celebrate myself for:

_____

_____

I forgive myself for:

_____

_____

Day 23

Affirmations - I AM:

_____

_____

Today I am grateful for:

_____

_____

Today I aim to:

_____

_____

Today I will practice self-care by:

_____

_____

Today I celebrate myself for:

_____

_____

I forgive myself for:

_____

_____

Day 24

Affirmations - I AM:

_____

_____

Today I am grateful for:

_____

_____

Today I aim to:

_____

_____

Today I will practice self-care by:

_____

_____

Today I celebrate myself for:

_____

_____

I forgive myself for:

_____

_____

Day 25

Affirmations - I AM:

_____

_____

Today I am grateful for:

_____

_____

Today I aim to:

_____

_____

Today I will practice self-care by:

_____

_____

Today I celebrate myself for:

_____

_____

I forgive myself for:

_____

_____

Day 26

Affirmations - I AM:

_____

_____

Today I am grateful for:

_____

_____

Today I aim to:

_____

_____

Today I will practice self-care by:

_____

_____

Today I celebrate myself for:

_____

_____

I forgive myself for:

_____

_____

Day 27

Affirmations - I AM:

_____

_____

Today I am grateful for:

_____

_____

Today I aim to:

_____

_____

Today I will practice self-care by:

_____

_____

Today I celebrate myself for:

_____

_____

I forgive myself for:

_____

_____

Day 28

Affirmations - I AM:

_____

_____

Today I am grateful for:

_____

_____

Today I aim to:

_____

_____

Today I will practice self-care by:

_____

_____

Today I celebrate myself for:

_____

_____

I forgive myself for:

_____

_____

Day 29

Affirmations - I AM:

_____
_____

Today I am grateful for:

_____
_____

Today I aim to:

_____
_____

Today I will practice self-care by:

_____
_____

Today I celebrate myself for:

_____
_____

I forgive myself for:

_____
_____

Day 30

Affirmations - I AM:

_____

_____

Today I am grateful for:

_____

_____

Today I aim to:

_____

_____

Today I will practice self-care by:

_____

_____

Today I celebrate myself for:

_____

_____

I forgive myself for:

_____

_____

I celebrate you for completing your Confidence MBA Challenge and unleashing a more confident version of yourself. Keep turning up the dial on your thermostat; discomfort is a part of the growth process.

"GROWTH IS PAINFUL. CHANGE IS PAINFUL, BUT NOTHING IS AS PAINFUL AS STAYING SOMEWHERE YOU DON'T BELONG."

Mandy Hale

NOTES

_____
_____
_____
_____
_____
_____
_____
_____
_____
_____
_____
_____
_____
_____
_____
_____
_____
_____
_____
_____
_____
_____
_____
_____
_____
_____

Made in the USA
Middletown, DE
24 October 2023

41338940R00040